D1091351

DISCARDED
UNIVERSITY OF WINNIPEG
LIBRARY
515 PORTAGE AVENUE
WINNIPEG, MAN. R3B 2E9

NEWS OF THE NILE

NEWS OF THE NILE

A BOOK OF POEMS

by
R.H.W. DILLARD

The old people in a new world, the new
people made out of the old, that is the
story that I mean to tell, for that is
what really is and what I really know.
Gertrude Stein

Meantime this earth of ours . . . is full
of wonders and mysteries and marvels, and
. . . it is good to go up and down seeing
and hearing tell of them all.
Rudyard Kipling

The University of North Carolina Press
Chapel Hill 1971

Contemporary Poetry Series

Manufactured in the United States of America
ISBN 0-8078-1162-9
Library of Congress Catalog Card Number 77-132251

Some of the poems in this volume have previously appeared in *The Mill Mountain Review, Modine Gunch, Fly by Night, The Roanoke Review, The Hollins Critic, TriQuarterly,* and *The Hollins Poets.*

FOR MY PARENTS
BENTON O. DILLARD
&
MATTIE MULLINS DILLARD

CONTENTS

OLD WORLD: grammar

NEW WORLD: geography

OLD WORLD grammar

Erthe took of erthe erthe with wogh;
Erthe other erthe to the erthe drogh;
Erthe laide erthe in erthen trogh:
Thanne hadde erthe of erthe erthe ynogh.

NIGHT OF THE LIVING DEAD

1.

Her lips were never near the blood. The tongue
was relatively long. It moved at the rate of
about four darts a second. At the instant of
protrusion it was pinkish, but once in action
it functioned so perfectly that a pulsating
ribbon of blood spanned the gap between the
surface of the fluid and the creature's lips.
—R. L. Ditmars & A. M. Greenhall
"The Vampire Bat"

Adam's fall lies on you
Like your own arm in the night,
Dead with your weight,
Heavy as your dream,
You heave to throw it off.

You see it in all things:
The goat's hot blood
And randy eye, tail
Of the lizard, raven's
Croak, the buzzard's meal,

Erosion, drought,
The plague, the rain
That does not wash it clean,
Tree's knot, bare wood
That rots and warps,
The tumor and the wound,
Necessity of blood.

Smear yourself with the hoopoe's blood
And you will dream of smothering devils,
Drink the blood of the beast
And be as strong as his dark heart,
Swallow the leech
And he will drain you dry.

The sun sets like blood,
Rises like blood,
Dry clay is the color of dry blood,
Sap flows in the spring like blood,
You cry like bleeding,
Your blood is as black as loam,
You are swollen with blood,
Yearn for the lancet, the bleeding cup.

2.

And so I muddied the clear spring
of friendship with the dirt of physical
desire and clouded over its brightness
with the dark hell of lust.
—St. Augustine
Confessions

You are quiet as a snake
In winter, coiled,
Your eyes as clear
As gem stones, as cool.

Who would suspect?

Hunched over her small bed,
You would lick her veins dry,
Have her in the winding sheet,
Pale as potato stalks in the dark room,
Still as basalt, as carved granite.

Your teeth ache like your nerves,
Heart's muscular desire,
Down to the root, like a small boy
Chewing grass in the frenzy,
Like a fallen fruit
Splitting in the day's heat.

The reptile's scar on your heel,
Crippled, you crave the bat's wing,
The sweet smell of its gorged sleep,
Night vision, the quick tongue.

And if her eyes prove red
As her swollen lips,
Her teeth sharp to your throat,
Her touch like the vampire's kiss,
Thirsty for the same raw drink,
You will empty like a shadow,
Shrill as a north wind, cold
As the coffin, dirt to dirt,
Try to cry out your name
And scrabble on the floor at dawn.

3.

The last glimpse I had was of the bloated face, blood-stained and fixed with a grin of malice which would have held its own in the nethermost hell.

—Bram Stoker
Dracula

You are howling like a dog,
You lick your own shame.

You are naked as a new day,
Shivering in the bright air.

The eye that stirred
Your pain is as common
As your own, as dull,
Her fingers, point
Of the hip, the wrist.

You are old meat,
Aware of each clogged cell,
The bruise that spreads
Beneath the skin,
Split tooth, shaved bone,
The liquid in your lungs.

Your lips are cracked
Like a dry river bed,
You are washed in blood,
Sluice of the pulse
That rushes in your ear,
Source of the open sore.

You dream of the coffin's lid,
The driven stake to cure
Your skinned heart, wolfsbane
And garlic, your head hacked off.

You are lonely as the lost wolf,
The slug, the blind whale.

A dove's feet are red
As fire, as spilled blood,
As its own hard eyes.

We once took hope
That the pelican was said
To feed its young
With its own red blood.

EVENT; A GATHERING; VASTATION

If the natural world is so double-faced and
unhomelike, what world, what thing is real?
—William James

Rolling in glass, drunk
As cauliflower, knowing
The flaw but not knowing
Its nature, swamped:

Blue as an old orange,
You grip the sash,
Hear the day like a noise
In an empty hall, warped,
Discolored, open, endless.

You have blown out the candle,
Taken the required beating,
Opened the gifts: raw knuckles,
Crisp skin, the bruise.

Old as any hour, eroding,
Caught in a mirror, thrown
Back bent and peeling,
You have celebrated too well,
Too soon, are alone too soon.

The old day mocks you,
Dies with the blind twist
Of a moth, flying by stars,
Downed by electric light.

And the night covers you up,
Small scars, the large deformity,
Leaves you on the rug, pinched
In your own shadow, a day
And years older, on a bed of shards.

ACT OF DETECTION

Being singularly free from the conventional
sentimentalities and current superstitions,
he could look beneath the surface of human
acts into actuating impulses and motives.
—S. S. Van Dine

The centipede, the spider,
Shark's head and beetle's
Shell, disordered room,
The mind at bay, the mind.

The fact of Bela Kiss:
Scorpio and Cancer, knot
Of the strangling cord,
Two dozen dead, two dozen,
Broken and floating in oil,
Preserved like foetal pigs,
Their throats cracked
Like ice, naked, female,
Their hair like pond scum.

Pull back the curtain,
Probe in the new dust,
Examine the surfaces,
Chair rungs, the mirror's
Back, chalk out the floor,
Dry out the corners
Of the room, and pry,
Pry at the corners, the seams,
The ravelling paper on the wall.

Think of the guillotine,
The headsman's ax, the rack,
The wheel, the lives
Of the saints, the hangman's
Noose; remember loud Jack
The Ripper, quiet Kürten,
And the sane assassins,
Guiteau and Czolgosz,
Booth's dangling leg.

Measure and reflect,
Examine the stiffness
Of the arm, eye's cast,
The burn, the stain,
Mashed roach and spider's
Sting. The mind at bay.

The quick mind, quick
As the centipede, the shark's
Hard thrust, circling
The room, the room, circles
The room, wall, curtain
And door, closed door,
Locked door, shut window,
Circles and bumps the mirror,
And sees the eye, bared
Tooth, the quick grimace,
Skull in the mirror, face,
The mind at bay, the mind.

ANOTHER LAST MILE

The inhalation
And a slow exhalation,
An occlusion, and the heart's squeeze,
The brain's air are slowed,
Are stopped.

A frail collection:
This web of motion, bone's
Arrow and the strung gut.

The last grey mile,
Slit and cuffed, no voice
In the throat, one
In the ear, the heels,
The heels.

Not even a tin cup's clatter,
Not even solace
In dimming the lights
Of the next county
Where it thunders
Through each dark house.

The brain's boil
Stirred out, the muscles
Betray, shame, die.

And the belly digests
Itself, the leg,
The guilty arm,
The eyes that saw,
The mouth that scorned.

Until sewn up
And potted, set out
Behind the low wall,
You are nightsoil,
Limed down, lungless,
Carbon and crawling earth.

AFTER THE ELECTION, A DRY SEASON

Toad sweat and wart water,
Old blister, the pond
Shrunk to its thick center,
Its broken bank, snake holes,
The jerked frogs and hard scum.

The autumn ducks fly by
Sun bound and water true;
The white fowl are dead
In ragged weed and dry dirt.
This water holds no sky.

FINANCE MINISTRY

The green papers of money,
The monies we closed in leather bags,
The fine print in the open ledgers
And the way she crossed her legs.

It was a fine revolution,
An advance in taste and sound,
I touched her ear and heard
The etched, intelligent curve
Of her legs, and saw easily
The coin of her open palm.

No one milled in the streets,
Set torch to glass or stone,
The president's home stood
All alone as we began and struck
An image, made our clever stand.

The wood of the table gleamed,
Nickel hard with lemon oil and mint,
Not a stain, only faint scars
Where the gold had bounced
And rolled, the clips on the papers
Of money had made a mark or two.
Obverse her face came back awry,
In the depths of the polish
It was reversed and bare.

There is a frank, uneasy calm tonight.
No wind stirs the branches,
As steady as coppery seaweed,
A deposit at the river's bank.
We must probably withdraw
To win again another time,
To gain another time to win.

I am sure of the feel of leather,
Stamped in the grain, her bonds,
Cold coins, the bounce of her hair,
My own demands and the obvious answer.
I have struck a bargain and a blow,
And now we will retire and disappear
Into the nearby jungle, green leaves,
Tender bark, the snake and poison darts,
The green papers of money.

THE RED DWARF AND THE GREEN

> "I find that I have neglected to explain
> the working of these interesting
> mechanisms that were telephonic,
> dictaphonic, telegraphic in one."
> —*The Moon Pool*

I have been reading A. Merritt this afternoon,
Watching the wind blow the sun down
To the western hills (casting back late light
Like a desperate anchor onto the eastern ridge)
And wondering about these interesting mechanisms.

Those glowing globes pulse and tingle,
And cool Rador appears to understand.
Yolara's voice, so beautiful and evil, registers
A colorful dance as I tremble and hear,
Lugur & the Shining One—the Dweller in the Pool.

The footnote on page 134 is no great help,
For it presupposes my knowledge of Hertzian waves
And the "elementary fact of physics."
I am baffled, too, because the house is empty
And there is no one to offer me aid.

The Silent Ones, old three, are bird and reptile,
Human in their sleep. Eyes open wise and wide.
They understand, but do not tell. They only stare.
And where in all this black world flecked and living
Do I find the crimson sea? No answers in the afternoon.

I do realize that "The 'crawling' colors which showed
Themselves at these times were literally the voice
Of the speaker in its spectrum equivalent."
O, Lakla, handmaiden of the Silent Ones,
Glow through these walls and help me out.

The sky is wet now and the sun nearly drowned,
The afternoon is lost, and so, I fear, am I.
Lugur and Double Tongue are running free,
Yolara's hissing hair, the frogs are silent still.
The Shining One will ride the moon this night.

THE AIR RAID WARDEN REMEMBERS HOW IT SEEMED TO BE

Everyone is bawling like a baby.
—Cpl. Irving Strobing
Corregidor

Now, we betray it
With each expression:

Ticket stubs, ration
Stickers, and stamps,
The small pasteboard
Red tokens, and the blue
Ones, a postcard,
The flattened tin, the fat,
The white hairnet
For safety, "let's take
A pokio at Tokio,"
The armband, a flashlight,
Her eager reply.

When the news came
It was always raining,
And faces leaked
Like skin peeling
After a day at the beach,
Were impassive
As old posters:
The gagged parrot,
A nurse, the listening walls,
The dangerous Jap.

At the movies
We saw Benito hung
Up with his love
Like a pair of wet nylons.

The gas mask in the closet
Had a filter clean
As new leaves,
As the flowers on her dress,
As the sun signalling
Through massed bombers.

The last spring
When the V-letters
Were photostats,
As gray as the grass
For weeks after
The first warm days,
The searchlights
Dimmed out, the blinds
Were spread. They sounded
The all clear.

THE DESTINY AT PLYMOUTH: 21 JUNE 1618

A meditation for George Garrett

We die in earnest, no jest,
Rawly like a bruise, flesh
From the withered tree, fruit
Of decay hung on the bone.

Wood and weed mark out the way,
Wag's way from sea to land,
Sheets wet, dust on the tongue,
And always dust to sea to dust.

The story of a day shut up,
Earth, grave and dust, a rattle
Like knuckles of a broken fist,
One last tattoo, no last delay.

So only trust remains, a dance
On sawdust, a way that times
Day to dusk to the edge of days
Where soil breaks green as a sea.

LOOKING FOR ASIA

You are out of the way to Japon,
for this is not it.
—Captain Luke Foxe (1631)

The bay is as cold
As colored silk at night,
As smooth as colored silk.

The two small ships hang
On their anchor lines
Like paper balloons,
Easing around in the tide,
Echoed in the still water.

Well into the long day,
The sun reaches for Japan
As it crosses the bay
And points the ships' masts
Back home across the water,
Across lost Vinland, the ocean,
The familiar tides of Bristol.

Captain Foxe offers his advice,
And the two captains laugh
Like the rattle of swords,
Tear the silent air
Like paper walls, secure
In having come beyond the point
Of Frobisher's return, where
Hudson's wake lingers
In the still cold water
Like an uneasy ghost.

We find the story
In *North-West Fox*, p. 223,
(1635). The captains' laughter
Eddies in the bay, mingles
With the sound of axes
On the shore, spattering
From the slim pines
Like small arms fire.

WHEN AND WHERE ARE OBELISKS WASHED AND ARCHES

"When and where are obelisks washed
And arches," with high thick suds
And stiff white brushes, the men
In blue coveralls and dark goggles
Scrubbing them down, the bubbles
Playing pale prisms on the old stones
And bouncing once on the cobbles and slate,
While a military band in shakos
And high black boots stands pat
Playing the traditional national air
To old men with rosettes and knobkerries,
The streets bent off into several ways
With lilies and roses of Sharon
Blooming in copper pots on the lamp posts,
And large men in Lincoln green overalls
Brushing the gray soapy water along the gutters
And into the drain, bare headed and silent,
As the faint hieroglyphs like dominoes
Come clean and clear in the afternoon
For those to read who can and care,
As the damp arches gleam overhead.

ON MYNYDD HIRAETHOG: AFTERNOON

For Ian & Kanta

On Mynydd Hiraethog high near Llyn Alwen
Where the hill peels off from the stone tower
And the stained glass creaks in the dark house,
The wind cracks the air like you would crack an egg,
Splits and separates it, lays the flat grass flatter
And makes a man lean heavy, angle out.
The rain comes in level, and you must turn
The top of your cap into it like a round tweed shield.
The windscreen wipers of your car slip through,
Only lead you blind to the edge of the road
And the moor sliding off under the gravel.
Denbigh Castle was in friendly hands, safe
With wide boards laid on the damp shirred stone,
And the Vale of Llangollen will be still
With chimney smoke hanging low and steady,
But on Mynydd Hiraethog the storm
Stirs Llyn Alwen into stiff froth,
Winds the dim hallways of the stone house
Shrill with the afternoon, whips clouds
Into flat rain, and forces you to faith,
Leaning down to sunset on the wind.

DELIVERING THE MAIL

At first, it is a delicate task,
The sorting out, the spreading,
The tips of the fingers, light
And deft, the nerves alert,
Opening the box, always aware
Of appropriate zones, the necessary code.

When everything is properly out
And all directions are clear,
You must place the mail in the pouch,
Which you have oiled and rubbed,
Kept firm and soft, supple
Without losing its shape.

Lay it in carefully and in order,
Carelessness at this juncture
Can spoil an entire day's work,
Cancel the best of plans,
Everything in as it should be,
In to be taken out, all in good time.

And then the tour itself,
Steadily through the whole route,
Moving in and out of the pouch,
Separating and putting it in the slot,
Each piece in its place,
Each item delivered home.

And now you can relax,
A job well done, first class,
In spite of driving rain, the sleet
Or hail, the mail delivered,
The post gone through, at ease,
And the pouch stored safely away.

HIS HAND, HER SCOTTISH WIZARD

For Judy and Betsy

Stirred like old milk,
The air of the eye
Hardens, lens tight,
The compulsive click.

The afternoon as clean
As silicone, as clear,
Pure, with blank leaves
Slipping the tree.

A development:
The white room, black
Curtains, window
Open out over the day,
The early evening
Diffuse as a red eye.

And the hand, open,
Held like his hand,
Her Scottish wizard,
A pinned leaf to the air,
The familiar reversals,
The turn of an eye.

Then the dark demand,
Threat of exposure,
A night acid
With an absence,
An understanding blurred,
An odd expression.

When the first owl
Shutters the spread moon,
A flying squirrel,
The window focussed
On the drying leaves,
The eye unfurls,
Strips the day
Into separations,
Steadies, is true,
Still as new cream.

THE GLASS DOG

Quanto tempo resteremo qui?
—G. de Chirico

Clear air is following
A true line
And a low lining,
True air and a long validity.

Motion informs a locomotive
Before a low moon,
Limned clear and along,
Lunar and an eyelid.

Scene with a new eye:
Motor ability and a fall,
Formal, lunatic, allow
A rising of the moon.

And the cloud of steam
Lime green, reformed,
Or a true clarity,
Malleable and modern.

Angry under a clear moon,
I lead, and she, mad,
Alone, agreeing, meets
The locomotive, the urn.

The dun hand in a round air
Lining her and the city,
Mills, dams, the small sea,
And the moon a clear motion.

MOBILIZATION

The line of beauty symbolizes motion.
—Bronson Alcott

Invisible like old trees,
An arc of birds, the thermometer,
A face, the familiar curve,

Words make new lines,
Die like oiled mosquitoes,
Seldom turn to a proper circle.

A bare wall, brick, the mortar
Splitting like skin, the nerve
Spread in a raw frame,

A steady hand must know
The aim, a flowing, shape
Of the eye, rolling, still.

Around the wire the coiled foot
Must hold, the arms may wave,
The ear hear the pluckt tone,

But balance depends alone
On sea sounds of the inner ear,
Moon drawn, swollen, round.

A bomb's path to earth
Is as well the plane's away,
A bullet's, the pitched ball's,

Fired out or thrown,
Dropped, the line is one,
Change slow, curve of a tear.

Flat on the screen, a cheek
Is flesh to thought, a porcelain cube
Curves on a larger screen,

Is as hard and plane to eye
As concrete to the hand,
For mind pays no mind to fact.

Visible as love's touch,
The shout, cut tree, dead bird,
The opossum by the porch step,

Words make old lines
Revive like warm turtles,
Bend to realize a move.

NEWS OF THE NILE

Don't all rivers flow south,
or is that just a common
misconception?

—Anonymous Student
20th Century

1.
The river Nile flows north from Khartoum,
Blue and white. Two rivers meet at Khartoum,
Mix between Tuti and Omdurman day and night
And flow north to wine dark seas, past these:

2.
Towns of the Nile:
Khartoum, trunk of the elephant, Atbara,
Fagrinkotti, Dongola, Kerma and Wawa;
Names now lost in Nasser's lake (Gebel Adda,
Dakka, Kabosh and Kalabsha); Aswan
And Kom Ombo, Luxor and Thebes, Sohag
And Mallawi, Biba, Badahl and Beni Suef;
Khartoum, where the Mahdi rules,
To Maadi where John Rodenbeck resides;
And, too, the delta's many jumbled towns.

3.
The fat man wears a tarboosh
Though his head seems made for fez.
He is standing at the elevator's doors.
He claps his hands and claps them
Once again. The only sound
That circles down the shaft
Is Fakkaruni. Um Kalsum is on
The radio.

4.
Cairo is a city of tall buildings,
Martian by a crow's choice, city
Red in the late sunlight, the Citadel
And Cairo Tower in the setting sun.
The taxis blow their horns. The Nile
Makes islands in its northern way.

5.
The music's high and loud, it has
No count in decibels, dark glasses
And hot coffee in the bar. The voice
Is Um Kalsum's. A fat man pauses
At the door and tilts his head.
The song is Fakkaruni. The sun is hot.
Dark glasses for the light is needle bright.

6.
The Nile flows north. A train runs north
From Roanoke to Chicago. The snow
Is like cold satin. There is a gibbous moon.
North to Chicago, towards Minnesota
Where the Mississippi oozes from a frozen bank
And wanders south, to Wisconsin
Where August Derleth prints the books
Of Lovecraft, dreamer of *The Book of Thoth,*
The Necronomicon, lost work of Abdul Alhazred,
Lovecraft who wrote of Nug and Dagon,
Old gods, Nÿogtha and Cthulhu.
And east of this train, south of Virginia,
In western North Carolina, Fred Chappell
Has written a novel, *Dagon,* and all these things
Come together, turn together, and will pass on
To come again. The Nile flows sluggish
And is thick with mud. It bears the news.

7.
The Nile has other names:
Kasumo and Kagira, Mukasenyi,
Ruvironza and Kagera, Nilus
And Ruvabu. The Nile, white and blue.

8.
A fat man in Chicago buys a ticket,
Walks into the darkness and sits down.
The Mummy's Curse is on a double bill,
The Mummy's Curse of 1945. The mummy,
His one hot eye that sees the ends of things,
Is Lon Chaney, and the fat man sweats
With fear, thinks of George Zucco,

Turhan Bey and Carradine. His palms
Are wet as Kharis seeks his revenge.
Anck-es-en-amon could live again;
Imhotep disguised as Ardath Bey
Attempts to steal her into life,
Worships Anubis, his jackel head,
But is destroyed by Isis, her potent rod.
The Mummy (1932), with Boris Karloff,
As the fat man clutches his left arm
And gasps. The Nile flows north,
Its banks weighted with temples,
Drinking the mud of their foundations.

9.
Gods of the old Nile, there are these:
Nun and Atum, Ra, Anhur and Shu,
Osiris, his wife Isis who is mother
Of all things (or was), Hathor who fed
Young Amenhotep as a cow, and falcon
Horus, Anubis and the baboon Thoth.
These and others, cat-headed Bast,
And Hapi (not Hapy, son of Horus,
But the dual goddess of the Nile),
All these and more. God bless
The reader of these names.

10.
The moon is high as the Nile is slow.
The snow is melting now in the dead
Of winter, but spring is still far away.
All these things I have read and remembered,
Witnessed, imagined, thought and written down,
Having ridden north on trains by day and night
With Henry Taylor to read our poems, listened
To recordings of Um Kalsum, dreamed of the Nile
And the moon dancing in dry palm fronds,
I, Richard Dillard, in this month of February, 1967.

NEW WORLD geography

Let us single out some Remarkables,
and glorify our God!
—Cotton Mather

AN AMERICAN FACT

An American fact: the Tong.

Observe the serious policeman,
His moustache, badge, his bowler
Hat, who walked Chinatown
In 1906 and lost the left side
Of his lonely face.

In the alleyway, behind the door,
Painted like a red Indian,
A yellow peril waits,
His hatchet sharp as a bat's ear.

In America. In San Francisco
Where the air is as cool
As banknotes, the days
Like silent hills. Skulls
Split as easily as a fresh
Deck, as firecrackers.

Not long ago.

Know that the past is never far:
Bone's blade, nerve's noose,
Tong of the broken blood,
Feel the bare soles in your skin,
The pigtail of your spine,
Your narrowed eye, clenched hand,
The gorge that clots your tongue.

DOWNTOWN ROANOKE

1.
The streetlights blink DONT WALK WALK
DONT WALK and the cars are filling
The air with burnt gas. And all will pass.
I often think and secretly suspect
Big Lick will come again and cows
Will graze in downtown Roanoke.

2.
A trip to the zoo: where we watch
The llamas chew and stare, stare
At the bears and pat the baby goats.
We walk by the crazy mirrors
Where we are stranger than the strangers
In the cages, furry and climbing
On the wire of their cages.
We ride the small train and wave
Out over the edge of the mountain,
Wave down at the valley, the puzzle
Of downtown Roanoke.

3.
The star on the mountain turns red
Whenever someone dies in the street,
But I have heard (although I have not seen)
That late at night in the earliest
Of morning, someone always turns
It red and then, I wonder, does
Someone gasp and stumble into a car
And die in downtown Roanoke?

4.
The mayor puffs on his cigar,
(The mayor is my dad), puffs
On his cigar, and the children
Dance around his legs, they sing
And toss petals in the smoky air,
And the mayor puffs on his cigar,
(The mayor is my dad), while people
Stare, he puffs, the little ones,

They dance and sing, the people
On the sidewalks think it strange, they
Do not understand in downtown Roanoke.

5.
From the airport the whisper jet
Rises on a wisp of black smoke
And a thunderous roar, draws me
To the door to observe. It is
A pale night and the lights
Of the plane are blinking green
And red. The star is white.
And the jet flies on while
The moon is full, as I think
Seriously of climbing in my car
And driving down 581 to see
The empty streets of downtown Roanoke.

6.
The Park and the Roanoke
And even the Rialto are parking
Lots. The Academy of Music
With its famed acoustics
Where Caruso and others sang
Is long down and gone.
There are many parking lots
And garages in downtown Roanoke.

7.
The Pakistani gentleman said,
In progress to a nearby college,
"I have lived in the vale of Kashmir
For much of my life, but I would
Gladly live and die in this valley."
The valley is green, the mountains blue,
All around downtown Roanoke.

8.
The furniture store across the street
From the main fire house has burned
Nearly to the ground three times.
The smoke hung low and red, the red
Stop lights blinked, but no sirens
Were required in downtown Roanoke.

9.
And when it rains, it pours water
In streams down the windows of the stores
And blurs the names, and down the windshields
Of heavy trucks and delivery vans. It wets
Down the dust and cleans the air and wets
The trainmen's high striped hats, makes
All the highways slick, and pours
Down all the undertakers' black umbrellas.
When it rains, the water runs down
The tombstones in each of the various cemetaries
And wears down the stone and wears down
The names into the ground where their dust
Lies. And when it rains, it wets the sides
Of buildings, and the building by the tracks
Built out of coal sheds long black streams
That crawl across the sidewalk, streak the gutters,
And run down the streets of downtown Roanoke.

10.
There was once a pool hall one flight
Down across the street from another
One just one flight up. The lower
One had a sign that read BILLIARDS.
The higher one is still there, one
Flight above downtown Roanoke.

11.
There are many birds in Roanoke.
I have seen: a great blue heron,
A green heron, the shy least bittern,
Orioles and robins, killdeers
Live near our house, and sandpipers,
Cowbirds who pick the dung of cows,
Wrens and sparrows, the familiar
Cardinals and blue jays, martins
And swallows, warblers make the air
Yellow in the spring, grackles,
A hundred cedar waxwings my mother found
Eating berries in a dogwood tree,
And towhees, nighthawks, and high
Overhead, their wings ragged
And spread wide, vultures, black
And circling over downtown Roanoke.

12.
My wife is from Pittsburgh.
Our dog is from Georgia. My friends
Are from New York and South Carolina,
Florida, Texas and northern Virginia,
Norfolk and even Connecticut.
My grandparents and parents
Are all from south of here,
From Franklin and Henry counties.
My wife says I am the only native,
That all the other inhabitants
Are castaways in downtown Roanoke.

13.
At early dusk in Roanoke the lights go on,
Neon, they're red and green, are purple,
Never gold, blink, stammer and fizz,
And say the names of things to people
Driving through, walking the streets,
On Pullmans in the railway yards
Waiting for the porter to make their beds.
The sign for YELLOW CAB is red and shines
Through white smoke to make the center
Of the city blaze like the mouth of hell
At early dusk. And outside the light
With only one red neon light at night,
The topless go-go girls lift up their knees,
They shake their breasts and do the frug
And bugaloo, they never smile, dance
In the dark beyond the light in downtown Roanoke.

14.
There is a blind lady with tilting
Scales on the seal and flag of Roanoke,
With steaming railroad trains
Shuffling at her knees. She appears
To be a young lady, and there is a great
Cogwheel or gear beside her.
The flag is blue. When they took
The one in the Council chambers
Down to make a copy, it fell
Into many pieces. One small piece
With one full pan of the blind lady's
Scales flew out of the window,

Across the lawn and into the traffic
Grinding gears in downtown Roanoke.

15.
We are watching the night, and the wind
Is very high. It strums the TV antenna.
It blows the dog's ears and makes
The windows rattle. The large highway
Signs hum in the wind. It makes
The heavy neon and steel star shake.
Perhaps it will accidentally turn
Red. It blows around and all round
The valley, wrinkling the new pale
Leaves on the trees, blowing
An occasional bird's nest over
And scattering the eggs. The wind
Blows up the streets and slaps
A bus transfer against the window
Of an elementary school principal's
House. She stops grading papers
And thinks of calling the police.
It rattles a paper cup up Jefferson
Street from the viaduct, a right
Turn onto Campbell Avenue, wrong
Way onto a one way street, turns left
On First Street at Fine's Men's Shop
And passing Kirk winds up in a storm
Drain at the corner of First and Church.
The wind blows the flat metal signs
On the side streets, blows grit
Into a rookie policeman's eyes.
He almost draws his gun but instead
Steps into the pool hall door. It blows
All up and down the streets, moans
In the halls of the empty office
Buildings, rattles the mayor's door,
And the door of my dentist next door,
And the door of the Office of Smoke Control.
The wind blows the mercury vapor lamps
That keep it always light in downtown Roanoke.

TRAVELOGUE

For Henry Taylor

There are things I have seen
Although I have not been
To where they are. They burst
In my skull like instant coffee
Flavor buds. My eyes spin
Like firework wheels, crackle
Like Frankenstein's machines.
I am ecstatic and grow
Electrically happy like cat's fur
Rubbed briskly backwards.

SALT LAKE

A little corner of Utah is soon traversed, and leaves no particular impressions on the mind.

—Robert Louis Stevenson

Where the mind tries to sink
But cannot, bobs up, dizzy,
Crusty, wrinkled, crystalline.

Afloat on the Salt Lake,
Feet crossed, exposed
Like confused icebergs,
Head back on a pillow
Of salt water, half asleep,
Dreaming of saline spectra
And the true way west....

The cut on your lip
Stings like the memory
Of rain; the locusts
Whir and split
Like late summer hail.
The seagulls scrape
As they circle
The encircled monument.

I have come in search
Of Eldorado which my friend
Poe indicated might be here
Where all the gold is soft
As lead and pure white.

You look vainly for waves,
Kick, crawl, stroke, scratch
Your skull on the hard water.

And then to awaken,
To wake up and take off,
Make the flat way to Nevada,
To Oasis, Deeth, Beowawe
And Lovelock.

And discover
That the grey surface
Of your mind is as smooth
As a balloon blown past
All trace of pucker.

THE UNKNOWN ESKIMO

These lonely latitudes do not belong
to the habitable world.
—Eugene Sue

The ground stiffens
Like arteries, trees
Like old toes, hard joints,
A wind shadowing the leaves
Across the day. Dead insects
Sting the sill. Light fails.

You feed the fire pages
Of last week's news, today's,
The wood damp as last week,
Cold as today.

North of Anaktuvuk, east
Of Point Barrow, the ice shifts
Like a dreaming animal,
Settles, solid as the soil,
As the sea below.

The sky is as lost
As the *Erebus* and the *Terror*.
The day disappears.

Think of the breath
Of caribou which hangs
For hours in the rigid air,
Of the unknown eskimo,
Of the polar bear, white
On a white plain, scenting
The hard white air.

EQUINOX

Instead of waiting for experience to come
at untoward times, he provokes it when it
can do no harm and changes the government
of his internal world accordingly.
—C. S. Peirce

An undone window,
A link in glass like onions,
The sea still as paper,
As an arm, as breath.

It is easier now,
Like reflections in snow,
The back arched as Tyre,
As levantine shadows.

So the ability to speak
Is as easily impaired,
We do not forget, only whisper,
Only walk, only forget.

A source, an attempt,
She ladders a garden,
Spreads fountains, sows,
Is the air of her eye.

With each sprout, a word,
A column like bedbugs,
Accidental, like loam
Along the shore, an alley.

Remembered like leather,
Or plastic, clasped,
We listen with spirit,
Splashing like bananas.

It is a good season,
Stretching like caged cats,
Like hemp, warm as a stroll,
New as an expression.

The sea moves like paper,
Provoked to an adjustment,
Secondary, tertiary,
The primacy of islands.

HOMAGE TO GERTRUDE STEIN

The asparagus
Is a green fountain
Through the open doorway,
Moving in the same air
That thrills the warm hair
Of your bare arm.

Here is a photograph:
First, the barbed point,
Honing the green grass,
Then the living shaft,
An unsupported spire.

And after slow rain,
A silent rush
And green mist.

This single photograph,
This open doorway.

WALKING HOME FROM THE RALEIGH COURT BRANCH PUBLIC LIBRARY

I reach the first real page
Of John H. Watson's reminiscences
Who took his degree in 1878.
The year is 1949, and I have only
A mile to go. I am walking home.

Sometimes today I want to loosen out
Like a large flag, possibly orange,
In an early April wind, and do.
But more often I remember
Walking home where I can really settle in.

OUR WEDDING JOURNEY

"Them birds went quack, quack, quack."

A voice, alone, the band had stopped,
The restaurant at the hotel's top,
(One last monument of architecture
Futuristic), with spiralled gutters
Down its sides, so smooth, and down
We slid, past pigeons, coos and
Strut, windows flitting past, light,
Dark, her naked breasts, his feet,
A shade, shadows, down and down, into

The city:
A doubledecker bus, red, curled
With long discarded tickets, stalled,
And in the street a dancing band,
Two men in sailor's suits, and one,
His concertina and his dancing shoes,
Gold-sprayed with wheels, golden
Roller skates, he danced, and off
The bus we stepped, gave him half
A crown in the shadow of Marble Arch.

The manor:
A diving tower, all steel and stone,
Pulling at the bars on the side
Of the wall, climbing to the tower,
And far below the pool, blue, empty,
Alone, although someone may be
Tipping at the top, leaning out
Ready to drop, on toes, arms out.

For dinner we had London broil,
With chips and peas, the same round
Peas we had before, with warm water
And a pot of tea. The band
Was stale, the floors polished,

The walls rounded at the corners,
The lights were round, bands of
Aluminium round the walls, the gutters
Outside ran round the building
And down, so smooth and round.
The band stopped, two dancers hung
Poised at the center of the floor,
A voice ran on and out:

"Them birds went quack, quack, quack."

ANNIE SLEEPING

She says that when babies
Are born, they are soft as milkweed,
Smooth as new berries,
Not shapeless like cubs, but soft,
Needing only to be licked by the air
To begin the callous of skin,
The hardening of breathing in
And breathing out.

And, too, each night or afternoon,
In sleep or nap, we slip back
Into darkness, away from air
And sun, and soften, round out,
Are buffed back to slow surfaces
And smooth lines. We do not break
The air but flow into the world.

And I can believe it with no qualm
Watching Annie sleep, a curve
Under the cover, a lump, her head
Beside the balled pillow, her hair
Astray, an arabesque.

And touch her as she sleeps,
Find faith, know waking can
Be cured, the rasp of air
Be healed. See with love's eye,
And like Thomas if you must,
Dare touch.

SINKING ROOTS

Our new house, wife and dog, ants,
Wasps, ticks who take their ticket
To ride the dog into our bed,
Visitors, and a lack of furniture,
Grading the same papers as before.

Thinking of sinking roots,
Lewd and frankly exploratory,
While three of our trees are dying,
But the others are opening out,
Taking their fill from the creek
And filling out the air with earth
Gone green and wide. Thinking of roots
And the fine hairs that divide
The soil lightly, tender,
And take it all in and up the trunk,
Drink the ground dry and leave
It to its inquiring worms.

Thinking of sinking roots
And staying awhile, propping
My feet up and watching the world
Turn the sun out at night,
Turning some words into a livelihood
Like water into trunk and vine,
Into bark and gum and leaves.

Leave veins to the sun,
Spread out and sink roots,
Fill out the empty house as well,
Chairs and machines, children,
Stacks of paper, thinking
Of sinking roots and settling in.

Considering whether they really did
Hang Huckleberry Finn as the hairball
Said for refusing to settle down,
To sink tough thirsty roots
In the soil of sivilization,
Not taking any chances, not I,
Am sinking roots and easing in
To where I know I ought to be.

MEDITATION FOR A PICKLE SUITE

Morning: the soft release
As you open a jar of pickles.
The sun through the window warm
And moving like light through brine,
The shadows of pickles swim the floor.
And in the tree, flowing down the chimney,
The songs of fresh birds clean as pickles.
Memories float through the day
Like pickles, perhaps sweet gherkins.
The past rises and falls
Like curious pickles in dark jars,
Your hands sure as pickles,
Opening dreams like albums,
Pale Polish pickles.
Your eyes grow sharp as pickles,
Thoughts as green, as shining
As rows of pickles, damp and fresh,
Placed out in the afternoon sun.

THE MULLINS FARM

The sun through the window
Is as warm as the smell of salt,
Of hams, the hum of bees
Where the smoke bellows lie
On the table by the netting,
The hat and the gloves.

My uncle hands you a turtle's heart,
Beating, beating in your open hand,
His head still hooked on the broom,
The hollow of his bones on the ground,
And his parts laid out by the fire,
The kettle made ready for soup.

The high horse, Mack, dappled white,
And the brown, too, slow and full,
The hill that falls off from the barn
Where the corn is husked in the dark,
And the hogs hanging to be split,
Filled with apples and corn and sweet slop.

By the branch out back and the small bridge,
In the damp concrete walls, the milk
Sits in spring water, and the squares
Of pressed butter, each with its bouquet
Of spring flowers, and on the bank,
An occasional frog or small snake.

The horseshoes must be bent on hot coals,
Red and white as new flowers, sprinkled
On the ground around the anvil, inviting
To your hand which must never touch,
And the shadows of the waiting horses,
The hot hammers, the hard men.

And the red hen in your arms is soft
And warm as the smell of feathers,
As the afternoon, while a small hawk
Watches from a crooked pine, watches
My grandfather in his clean tan clothes
Load his shotgun in the porch's shade.

And my grandmother rings the wood stove,
Takes the biscuits from the high warmer,
Calls her daughters to set the table,
And feeds the large family with squirrel
And green beans, squash and mashed potatoes,
As a brace of dead crows hang from the fence.

The afternoon is unending and clear
As the branches in front of and behind
The white house, as you climb the hill
To the barn, smell the stacked hay,
Touch the smooth wood of the stalls,
And see the sun powdered by barn dust.

My grandfather has cut a log of green wood
And set it up in the fireplace
With dry props to light as the evening
Comes on, and you may sit in the dim room
With the shadows wrinkling your face,
Hear the fire living in the light's slow leak.

The hounds are asleep on the front porch,
Their flat brown ears and sharp ribs,
While the cats climb to eat on a fence post,
And the oaks rattle acorns in the grass
And on the tin roof of the porch,
And the corn stalks crack in the air.

A CHILDREN'S HOUR: 1960

For Alice & Mary Gore

So it is grave Alice again
And Mary, laughing as she must,
Blue-eyed banditti, here
To prove that life does copy art
Even if the names are changed.

And they are giving me a picture,
(That's still clear; I have the proof),
A picture in pencil on a napkin,
Giving me a picture of me receiving
A picture which they are giving me
Like the one they are giving me,
Like the bottomless picture
Inside the picture (& the picture)
On the cover of a certain Captain Marvel
Comic book which I lost at last in 1953,
Opening in to the center of things.

Caught, pencilled in the act,
Hand up, reaching, on the take,
I promised then and tried
To pay proper credit for the day,
But only confessed that pose was mine,
Was clearly me, the hand, the nose,
And all the witnesses had agreed,
And here, years later, looking back,
Looking at an old page & into that sketch,
I surrender, like Proust and Keats,
Make the day bright again
To memory and in deed, I do:

For that look at the outside
That riffled in and in
Like a sharp's trick deck,
For quick Alice and Mary, this gift.

And thanks for the memory.

DOVE IN THE LEAVES

For Jim Seay

Not for everyone to find
In the lone tree of your new book,
Slick green like a new green leaf.

The dove's spring feathers
Puff pink against the dovey shadows
Of the tree.

Your new book, like a dove
In a lone tree, startles like a new leaf,
Familiar and strange.

The dove watches the course
Of the day, the sun, a passing
Idle hunter.

Do not bother to search
The contents (with numbers like spring leaves)
For the dove in your new book.

The dove observes languages
We are not born to, murmurs
Like a cool breeze.

Like a dove, your new book
Has a hold on air, on life,
On leaves from a deeper wood.

AND THEN THERE WERE NONE

A Love Song for the Accidentals

The days are as warm as eyebrows,
The bird seed we scattered sprouting
A faint green in the uneasy grass.

The notes of a day are round
As new buds, as a carving,
As voices over straw, over water.

Like ripples in a fresh pond
Opening out from the black duck,
They line the living air.

The past rises like a strange linoleum,
A hand in hand in hand, the harmony
Of clouds in the west, of twine.

These faces, reduced to essentials,
Unfold to the eye, to the ear,
A deck of colors spread in your hand.

The songsmith works away
At the tin piano, the organ stops,
An intrusion of voices, voices.

They form a circle as full
As winter, taut as spring,
Sudden as fall, as delicate as July.

And when we search the room
And find there are none, the sound
Will remain sure as dust, as dawn.

A DAY, A COUNTRY HOME

Homage to Vladimir Nabokov

This true estate:

There is time here for the sea
To die in waves slow as eyes,
Where the sound of each dying
Holds to the ear like hunger.

You walk along the pebbles
Of the shore. The high leaves
Lap at the late sun like dogs
Hot from the romp, the chase.

The water moves like a freed circle,
Spiralling into froth, into foam,
As the stone darkens and gleams
At each departure, wave on wave.

Is there a house through the trees,
Catching light through the leaves
Like butterflies, like the sun
Too bright to see, like the day?

You see two figures far down the shore,
A young man, his young blond wife,
Examining the stones, pocketing
A few bright pebbles, watching you.

The sun touches the edge of the day
As gingerly as hands, as fingers,
Your shadow slips long into the aspens,
Into their shade, clear to the golden walls.

A POETRY OF THE ACT

For W. R. Robinson

It's like riding a hot horse
Into high breakers, foam
On foam. You are wet
Through and through, and thrown
By horse and sea, laid out
On the sand, pushed in,
The undertow sucks only
At your feet and knees, winded,
Dazed, happy, as the horse
Stands shivering by the piled rocks.

ALLIGATOR NIGHT

1.

> *The horrid noise of their closing jaws,*
> *their plunging amidst the broken banks*
> *of fish, and rising with their prey some*
> *feet upright above the water, the floods*
> *of water and blood rushing out of their*
> *mouths, and the clouds of vapour issuing*
> *from their wide nostrils, were truly*
> *frightful.*
>
> —William Bartram

Alligator night, the moon
Mottled, scaled, the water
As still as old age, palms
Clack and chatter, the fish
Rise and fall in clear rings,
And the alligators slide
Down the mud, toes and sharp
Tail, move into the bay.

The eye of the reptile
Winks like the moon
Through thin clouds,
Is cold as a dead bird,
Will not leave you
To the dark alone.

Like old logs bumping
Down to the mill,
A dark convoy, secret
Submarines, the brothers
Of the sick shark,
The alligators come,
A symmetry, hungry order,
The one equation.

They scrub the planks
Of your boat, the hiss
Of their passing eyes,
Slick coins, tails
Stirring the bay water
Like scalding coffee,
A silence loud as artillery,
As a saint's death.

2.

For we are not pans and barrows, nor
even porters of the fire and torch-bearers,
but children of the fire. . . .
—R. W. Emerson

Seed case and tidal water,
Hard as blood, you strike
Nail on stone and blossom
Into sulphur, into flame,
Blaze and sputter, hot fat,
Break light from your dark cells.

A flame casts shadows,
Hisses, snaps, slips
Smoke into the night air,
And eats away, like cancer
Gnawing on old bones,
Bruised flesh, heat
Of decay, the growth
Under your arm, hot
Tumor snarled in your brain.

And die,
Old web, worn out,
An echo in his eyebrow,
Cast of her eye, a trunk
Of suits, the medal,
A husk as dry as kindling,
As tinder, punk.

3.

...children of the fire, made of it,
and only the same divinity transmuted
and at two or three removes, when we
know least about it.
—R. W. Emerson

After this sight, shocking and tremendous
as it was, I found myself somewhat easier
and more reconciled to my situation.
—William Bartram

There are cures:
The harsh salt, the acid,
Sharp knife, X-ray,
The pills and bitter capsules,
Tubes, pulleys, the plastic
Arm, the borrowed heart.

And in the ashes, old fire,
You stir like a stiff bird
At dawn, stretch out,
And try your hurt, gland's
Drain, eye's squint, locked knee,
Burn in the healed nerve.

The day like a lizard
Swells in the sun, colors,
The bay empty as glass,
Palms like feathers,
The light as round
As a button, as a day,
As open.

The alligator in the park,
No sign in his grey skin
Of breath, his one eye
Closed, warm in a circle
Of pond and high fence,
Sleeps in the sun
Like a painful memory.